LIVING WITH
EPILEPSY

Patsy Westcott

WAYLAND

Titles in the series

Living with Asthma

Living with Blindness

Living with Cerebral Palsy

Living with Deafness

Living with Diabetes

Living with Down's Syndrome

Living with Epilepsy

Living with Leukaemia

Series editor: Carron Brown
Book editor: Alison Cooper
Cover design: Steve Wheele Design
Inside design: Peter Laws
Consultants: Nick Tapp, East Sussex Disability Association, and
Sue Mitchell, British Epilepsy Association

First published in 1998 by Wayland Publishers Ltd
61 Western Road, Hove, East Sussex BN3 1JD, England

Find Wayland on the Internet at http://www.wayland.co.uk

British Library Cataloguing in Publication Data
Westcott, Patsy
    Living with Epilepsy
      1. Epilepsy – Juvenile literature
      I. Title II. Epilepsy
      362.1'96853

ISBN 0 7502 2249 2

Printed and bound in Italy by G. Canale & C.S.p.A., Turin

Acknowledgements
The publishers would like to thank Jackie Ditonowicz for her assistance, and the following for allowing their pictures to be used: Getty Images 8/Stewart Cohen, 12 (left)/Demetrio Carrasco, 12 (right)/Tim Brown, 26/Andy Cox; Angela Hampton Family Library Pictures *cover* (inset), 9; Science Photo Library *cover* (inset), 15/CC Studio, 16/Scott Camazine, 17/Will & Dent McIntyre, 20/James King-Holmes, 21/Alexander Tsiaras; Wayland Picture Library 7 (top)/APM Studios, 27/A. Blackburn, 28, 29; Tim Woodcock Photo Library *cover* (main picture)/Harry Graham. All the other photographs were taken for Wayland by Angela Hampton. Thanks to West Sussex County Library Service for help with photo shoots. The illustration on page 6 is by Michael Courtney. Most of the people photographed in this book are models.

Contents

Meet Naomi, Jessica, Tom and Joe

Naomi, Jessica, Tom and Joe are children like you. They live in homes a bit like yours, with their families. They go to schools like yours and have friends, just like you.

Naomi's hobby is mountain-biking. She likes to ride around with her friends, and at weekends she goes biking in the countryside with her mum and dad.

▽ Naomi enjoys going out on her bike.

Jessica loves animals, and she has a cat called Tiger. When she grows up, she would like to be a vet.

◁ Jessica has looked after Tiger since he was a kitten.

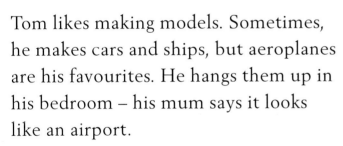

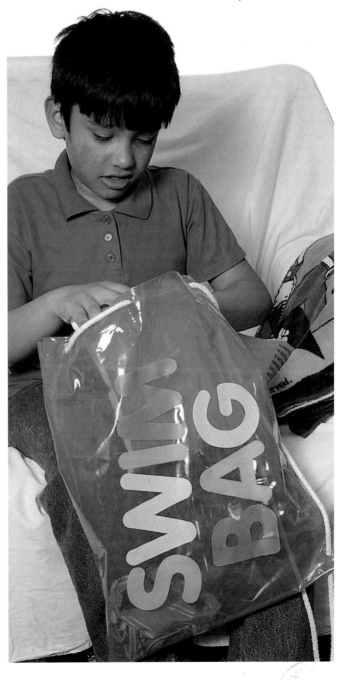

△ Tom would like to make real aeroplanes when he grows up.

▽ Joe has just joined the swimming club at the local pool.

Tom likes making models. Sometimes, he makes cars and ships, but aeroplanes are his favourites. He hangs them up in his bedroom – his mum says it looks like an airport.

Joe loves swimming, and he goes to the pool every week. He has a great time on the water slides.

Naomi, Jessica, Tom and Joe have different interests, but they have one thing in common – they all have epilepsy. This book explains what epilepsy is and how it affects people who have it.

A blip in the brain

You can't tell if someone has epilepsy by looking at him or her. You can only tell if he or she has something called a seizure. A seizure is a blip in the brain.

Your brain controls your body. It tells your heart to beat, it tells your stomach to digest food, it tells you to breathe. When you switch on the television it's because your brain has sent a message to your finger, telling it to press the button.

▽ Different parts of the brain control everything your body does.

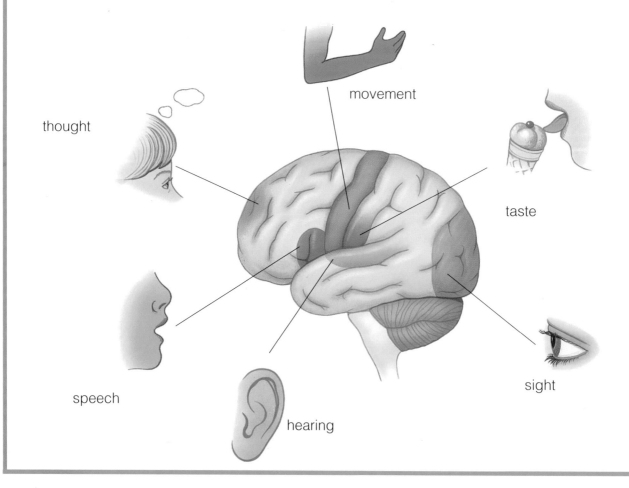

thought

movement

taste

speech

hearing

sight

▽ People often feel strange just before and after a seizure.

If someone has epilepsy, his or her brain sometimes sends messages so fast that the messages get muddled up. When this happens, the person may fall over and his or her mind may go blank. He or she may feel strange, or act in a strange way. This is a seizure. You may hear it called a fit, a turn, an attack, a funny spell or a black-out, but the proper word, the one that doctors use, is 'seizure'.

A seizure only lasts for a few seconds or minutes. For the rest of the time the person's brain works perfectly normally. The fact that Naomi, Jessica, Tom and Joe have seizures doesn't stop them enjoying life and doing things that other children do.

▷ Naomi and her friends enjoy using the computer at school.

Why epilepsy happens

Anyone can develop epilepsy. Babies, children, teenagers and grown-ups can all have it. The most common times for epilepsy to develop are during childhood, or when a person is over 65 years old. Sometimes, people with epilepsy have other problems that affect their brains. Joe was born several weeks too early. Although he was well looked after by the doctors and nurses, his brain did not get enough oxygen and was damaged. Because of this damage, Joe has learning difficulties, as well as epilepsy.

▷ A hospital doctor checks a premature baby. Problems at birth can sometimes lead to epilepsy.

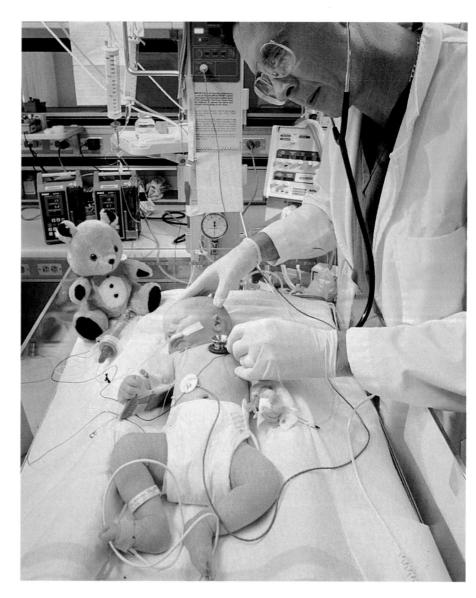

People who have hurt their heads badly in accidents sometimes develop epilepsy. Jessica developed epilepsy when she was three, after she was in a car accident. Epilepsy can also come on after a serious brain infection such as meningitis. This is what happened to Naomi. Some people have a family tendency to have seizures. In other words, if a child's parent or other relative has epilepsy, there is a chance that the child will develop it, too.

▷ Sometimes, people are more likely to develop epilepsy if a parent or other relative has it.

However, in most cases doctors don't know why a person develops epilepsy. Tom wasn't born early, he wasn't in an accident, he didn't have meningitis and there's no one in his family with epilepsy.

Seizures

There are many different kinds of seizure. Some people have more than one type, at different times.

When Naomi has a seizure she falls down on the floor, her body goes stiff and her arms and legs jerk. Sometimes she bites her tongue and quite often she wets herself. Naomi doesn't know this is happening to her and there's nothing she can do to control it. The seizure only lasts for a few minutes, but she feels quite confused and sleepy afterwards, and often has a headache. Seizures like these are the most common type – Joe has this type of seizure, too. They are called tonic-clonic seizures; some people call them 'grand mal'.

△ Naomi often sleeps for a long time after a seizure. She feels fine when she wakes up.

◁ Jessica always has someone with her while she is having a seizure, to make sure she is safe.

Jessica has a different kind of seizure. She doesn't fall to the ground, as Naomi and Joe do. Instead, she stops what she is doing and stares. Seizures like this are called 'absences', although you might hear people call them 'petit mal'. Jessica's seizures only last a few seconds, but while they are going on she doesn't know what is happening or where she is.

Many people don't feel anything while they are having a seizure, but some have a strange feeling. Jessica says, 'It feels like a jelly in your head.' Tom says he feels as if he's spinning round. When he is having a seizure he plucks at his clothes.

▽ Tom feels dizzy when he is having a seizure.

Triggers and warnings

Often, seizures just happen, but sometimes something sets them off. Some people have seizures if they have too many late nights and don't get enough sleep. Others get them if they are ill with a high temperature. A few people – but not very many – have a seizure if they see a flickering light, for example, from a television or a computer screen. All these things are called triggers.

Flashing lights in a club (below left) or a flickering computer screen (below right) can sometimes trigger a seizure.

Sometimes, people have a warning that they are about to have a seizure. They smell a funny smell, get butterflies in their tummy, or experience a strange feeling. Warning signs like these are called auras.

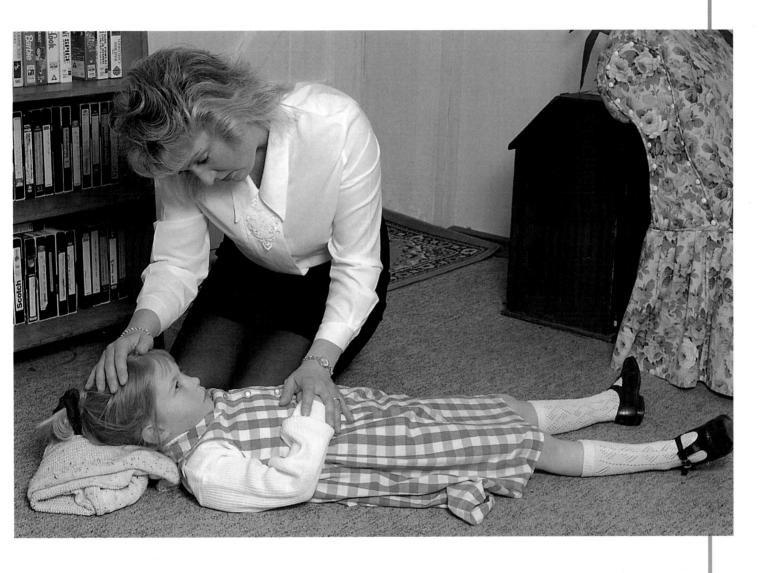

If a member of your family has epilepsy, you probably know what to do if he or she has a seizure. But if you see someone having a seizure and you don't know what to do, the best thing is to dial 999 and ask for an ambulance. Remember, there's nothing you can do to stop the seizure. Stay with the person until it is over, or until help arrives. Move things like chairs and sharp objects out of the way. Never try to put anything into a person's mouth during a seizure. When the seizure is over, try to roll the person on to his or her side.

△ Use a soft cushion or folded clothing to protect the person's head during a seizure.

Finding out about epilepsy

The first time Tom had a seizure his parents were very worried. They didn't know what was happening to him. They took him to the doctor, who sent Tom to see a neurologist at the hospital. A neurologist is specially trained to treat problems that affect the brain, although children are sometimes treated by a paediatrician instead. The neurologist decided to do a test called an electroencephalogram, or EEG, to find out if Tom had epilepsy.

▽ The neurologist explained that he thought Tom might have epilepsy.

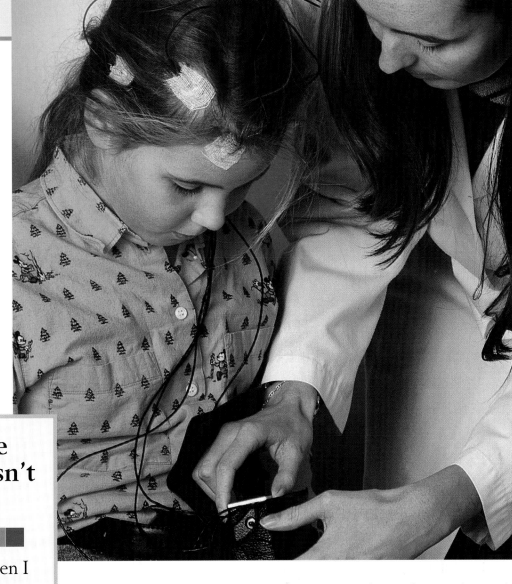

▷ This girl is having an EEG to pick up messages from her brain. Tom had this test, too.

Having the EEG test wasn't scary

'It didn't hurt when I had the EEG test, but it was a bit itchy. I had to sit very still and I really wanted to scratch my head!'

Tom sat in a chair and a nurse stuck sticky pads with wires attached to them to his head. The pads picked up messages being sent out by his brain. These messages passed through the wires to a machine which printed out a line on a piece of paper.

When the neurologist looked at the pattern made by the line, he was able to tell that Tom had epilepsy. He talked to Tom and his parents about the best way to treat it. A specially trained epilepsy nurse gave them lots of helpful information, too.

Having a scan

Having an EEG is one way to find out if a person has epilepsy. Another way is to do a scan. Having a scan doesn't hurt. The person having the scan lies flat on his or her back on a bed. The bed moves into the scanner, which looks a bit like the drum of a washing machine. When the top half of the person's body is inside the scanner, his or her head is held in place, to keep it still during the scan.

The scanner takes X-ray pictures of the brain, and a doctor uses a computer to make a picture of the brain appear on a television screen. He or she can see whether any areas of the brain are damaged in a way that causes epilepsy. This sort of scan is called a CT scan.

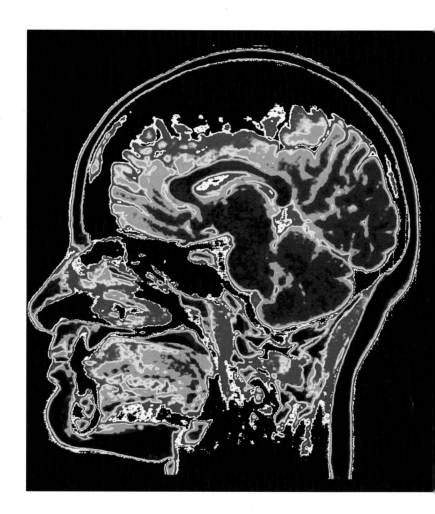

▷ This is a picture of a healthy brain, which has been produced by an MRI scan.

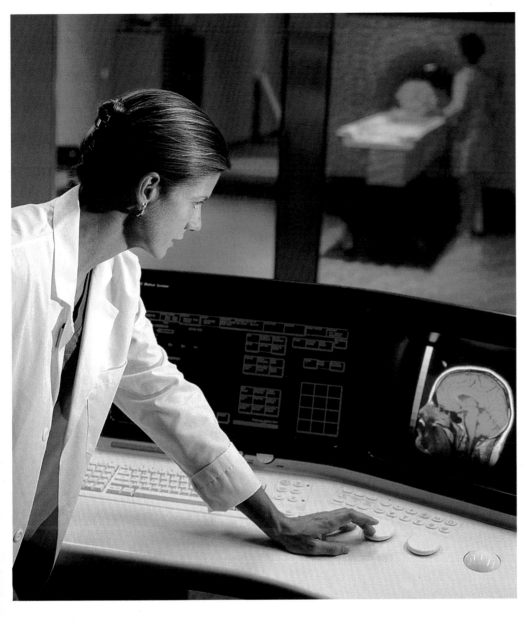

◁ In this picture someone is having an MRI scan. You can see the scanner in the background. The doctor is checking the image of the person's brain on the computer screen.

Another type of scan that people can have is called an MRI scan. In this sort of scan a very strong magnet is used to pick up signals from the person's brain. These signals are fed into a computer and a picture of the person's brain comes up on a computer screen. You don't feel as if you are being pulled by a magnet when you have this sort of scan, but it can be very noisy.

Controlling epilepsy

Naomi, Jessica, Tom and Joe have to take medicines every day to control their epilepsy. The medicines help to control the blips in their brains that cause seizures. Most people stop having seizures altogether, as long as they take their medicine.

There are lots of different medicines that can be used to treat epilepsy. Sometimes it takes a while to find the medicine that is best for a particular person. When Naomi first started taking her medicine, she felt tired and a bit sick. She found it hard to concentrate on her school work because she felt poorly.

It's quite common for people to feel like this to begin with, but these side-effects usually stop within one or two weeks. If the side-effects don't go away, the doctor can alter the dose or change the medicine.

◁ Naomi takes tablets every day to control her epilepsy.

My epilepsy is under control now

'The medicine I was taking at first made me feel really tired and sick. So the doctor decided to give me a different one. It took a while to get used to taking medicine every day but I'm used to it now. I feel fine and I haven't had a seizure for two years.'

△ Now Naomi's epilepsy is under control, she is feeling better and doing well at school.

Having an operation

Most people with epilepsy can be treated with medicines to prevent them from having seizures. But for a few people, treatment with medicines doesn't work. Sometimes, these people can have an operation instead, to try to stop them having seizures.

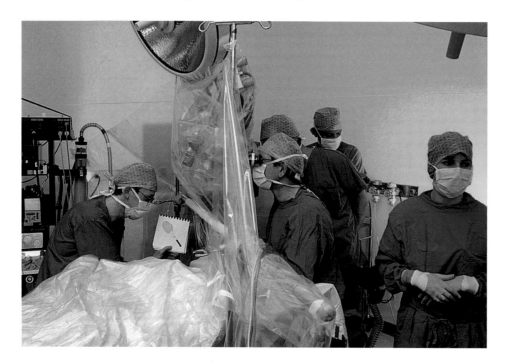

◁ This woman is having a brain operation to treat epilepsy.

Doctors who carry out operations on the brain have to be very skilled to make sure that they don't damage the brain. The doctor cuts through the skin and bone very carefully to get to the person's brain. When he or she has carried out the operation, the skin is stitched back together again and the wound heals. The only sign that the person has had an operation is a small scar, and this gradually fades.

Some surgeons are trying out new ways of doing brain operations, using a special light beam called a laser. This sort of operation can be done without opening up the person's skull. This means that there is not even a scar to show that he or she has had an operation. Another new way of helping people with epilepsy is to put a small gadget called a vagal nerve implant into their chest. The implant works on the nerves that cause a seizure.

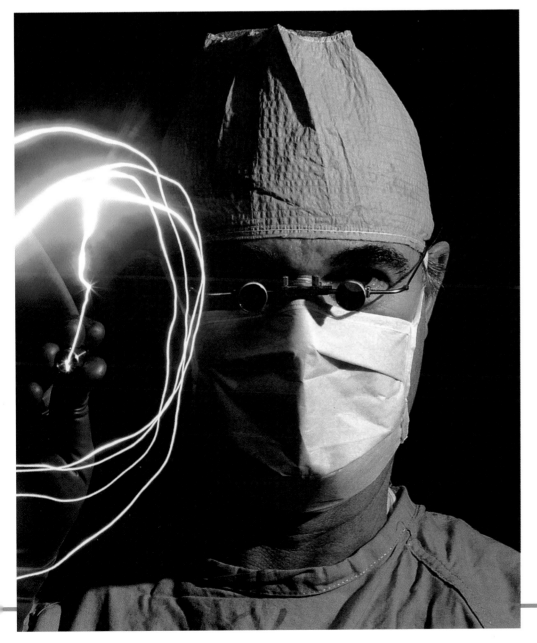

◁ This is a special light beam called a laser. It is sometimes used in brain operations.

Everyday life

One day, Jessica told the epilepsy nurse at the hospital about the way her mum and dad tried to protect her all the time. They were afraid to let Jessica go out without them, in case she had a seizure. They would only let her go on school trips if one of them came along too. Jessica didn't like her mum and dad making such a fuss. Some of the children at school had started making fun of her.

▽ Jessica was able to talk to the epilepsy nurse about the problems she was having.

The epilepsy nurse talked to Jessica's parents. She explained how important it was for Jessica to join in activities with her friends. She also introduced them to other parents whose children had epilepsy.

Talking to other people helped Jessica's parents to feel more relaxed. They let Jessica go out with her friends a lot more.

◁ Jessica is allowed to go to the playground with her friends now.

Please don't make a fuss!

'I got upset when mum and dad wouldn't let me do things. But last summer, they said I could go camping with my best friend and her family. I had a great time.'

▷ Jessica is looking forward to her next camping trip.

23

Problems at school

Most children with epilepsy go to ordinary schools. There are probably several children at your school who have epilepsy.

▷ Joe has a special teacher to help him with his school work.

Joe has learning difficulties as well as epilepsy. Joe was born early and his brain did not get enough oxygen and was damaged. His epilepsy and his learning difficulties are caused by this damage. When he started school, it took him longer than other children to learn to read, write and do maths. He has a special teacher who spends an hour a day with him at school, helping him with his work. This helps him to keep up with the rest of his class.

Once, Joe had a class teacher who didn't know much about epilepsy. He wouldn't let him use the computer, in case the flickering screen triggered a seizure. He wouldn't let him go swimming either, in case he had a seizure in the water.

Joe's parents went to the school to talk to his teacher and explained all about epilepsy. Joe's teacher realized that there was no reason to treat him differently from the other children.

▽ Joe's parents told his teacher all about their son's epilepsy.

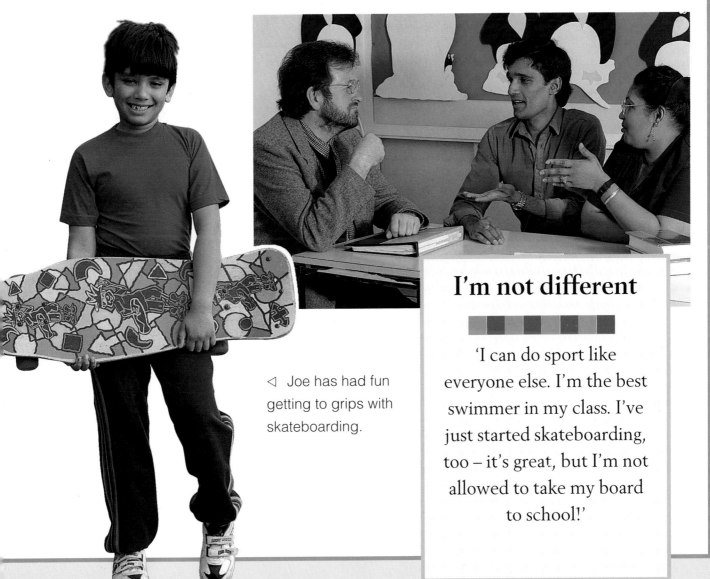

◁ Joe has had fun getting to grips with skateboarding.

I'm not different

'I can do sport like everyone else. I'm the best swimmer in my class. I've just started skateboarding, too – it's great, but I'm not allowed to take my board to school!'

Looking ahead

Many children who have epilepsy grow out of it as they get older. Even when people continue to have epilepsy, it doesn't usually stop them from getting on with their lives.

There are people with epilepsy in all walks of life. You might have seen some of them on television – some pop stars, TV presenters, sportsmen and sportswomen have epilepsy. Of course, most people with epilepsy are ordinary people. They are able to get jobs and can look forward to a future with children of their own.

▷ Babies and young children who have epilepsy may grow out of it as they get older.

△ People whose epilepsy is controlled by medicine are allowed to drive a car.

There might be a few jobs that people with epilepsy are not allowed to do, depending on the laws of the country where they live. If their epilepsy is under control, they are allowed to drive a car. (There are different laws about this in different countries, too.) The biggest difference between them and people who do not have epilepsy is that they have to take medicine every day.

Naomi, Jessica, Tom and Joe do not want people to feel afraid, embarrassed or sorry for them because they have epilepsy. What they do want is for people to understand a bit about epilepsy and what living with epilepsy is like.

Getting help

If you, one of your friends or someone in your family has epilepsy, there are several organizations that you can contact. They will be able to give you advice and information, and might be able to put you in touch with other people who have epilepsy.

The British Epilepsy Association (BEA) has been working for many years to improve life for people with epilepsy, and to help other people to understand what living with epilepsy is like. It produces helpful booklets, leaflets and videos, and it has local branches in most parts of the UK. You can write to the BEA at Anstey House, 40 Hanover Square, Leeds LS3 1BE, or you can ring the helpline (0800 30 90 30). Calls to this number are free. You can also contact the BEA's website (www.epilepsy.org.uk).

△ If you have epilepsy, it can help to talk to someone who understands what having epilepsy is like.

The National Society for Epilepsy is another organization that helps people with epilepsy. Its address is Chesham Lane, Chalfont St Peter, Bucks SL9 0RJ. The telephone number is 01494 601300.

Many hospitals have epilepsy nurses. These nurses are trained to help people with epilepsy and their families. They often go into schools to teach children about epilepsy, too. For more information about their work, you can contact the Epilepsy Specialist Nurse Association, Royal Liverpool Children's Hospital, Alder Hey, West Derby, Liverpool L12 2AP. (If you have specific queries about treatment, you should contact your local nurse through your hospital.)

There may be organizations in your area where people with epilepsy can share their experiences and get advice. Look in the phone book, contact your local Citizen's Advice Bureau (the address is in the phone book) or ask at your local library.

Glossary

Absence A kind of seizure in which a person's mind goes blank and he or she stares. It usually affects children and teenagers, and is also known as petit mal.

Aura The warning signs that some people get when they are about to have a seizure.

Brain An organ inside the head that controls everything we do, by passing messages to the nerves.

CT scan Computerized Tomography scan.

Dose The amount of medicine that has to be taken.

EEG A test that records the electrical messages sent out by the brain, to try to pick up any abnormal activity. EEG is short for electroencephalogram.

Epilepsy A condition caused by chemical disturbances in the brain, which cause seizures.

MRI scan Magnetic Resonance Imaging scan.

Nerves A bundle of fibres that pass messages through the body, telling it what to do, when it is moving, or how something feels.

Oxygen A gas that people take in from the air when they breathe. People cannot survive without oxygen.

Paediatrician A doctor who is specially trained to treat health problems affecting children.

Seizure A problem caused when messages being sent to the brain get muddled up. There are several different types of seizure.

Side-effects Medicines sometimes have unpleasant effects, as well as helpful ones. The unpleasant effects are known as side-effects. Doctors try to find the right balance between good and unpleasant effects, by trying different types of medicine.

Tonic clonic A type of seizure in which the person falls down and his or her body jerks. It is the most common type of seizure, and it is also known as grand mal.

Trigger An event that makes something else happen. Triggers for seizures can include alcohol, stress, boredom, late nights and lack of sleep.

Further information

Hand in Hand by Dr Richard Appleton (Hoechst Marion Roussel)

The Illustrated Junior Encyclopaedia of Epilepsy, edited by Richard Appleton (Roby Education Ltd, 1995)

Roby Education Ltd publishes a number of books and leaflets about epilepsy for children. For a list write to 3 Lyndhurst, Maghull, Merseyside L31 6DY.

My Mum has Epilepsy by Karen Llewellyn (Karen Llewellyn, 1994)

The Epilepsy Specialist Nurse Association has information packs for use in schools and by individuals. For details see page 29.

Further information about leaflets, books, tapes and videos is available from the organizations listed on pages 28–9.

Index